THE
SMART GUIDE
TO GETTING DIVORCED

What you need to know to be safe,
to be smart and most importantly—
to start your new life

PAUL STALEY

ISBN-10: 1475176619
ISBN-13: 9781475176612
Library of Congress Control Number: 2012907010
CreateSpace Independent Publishing Platform
North Charleston, South Carolina

DEDICATION

This book is dedicated to my to my clients, the first of whom nearly twenty years ago bore with me as I navigated a steep learning curve figuring out how to solve their problems; to the mentor attorneys – most notably Gordon Cruse – who, along with other generous veterans of family court gave unselfishly of their time to this then-younger protégé; and to the mental health professionals – most especially Ruth Roth, Ph.D. and Penny Angel-Levy - who have supported my clients and taught me invaluable lessons in the process.

ACKNOWLEDGMENTS

My thanks to the editors who, in short order, cured me of any no-tion that I could have foregone their employment. Without them, this first-time author would have missed countless lapses where his brain got ahead of his hands in producing this book.

CONTENTS

PREFACE

When you got married, you likely did not spend much time thinking about what it would take to end your marriage. Yet for many reasons, almost half of marriages *do* end. Whether or not you have children, the way you choose to end what began out of love can leave lasting imprints on everyone involved for better *and* for worse.

When things go wrong in a marriage, they can build up slowly over time or happen suddenly. Maybe you feel that both of you are responsible; maybe you blame each other. Either way you want a better future. You want to make sure that how you bring your union to a close puts you on a healing course to begin the next part of your life's journey. You want to be safe. You want to be secure. You want to be smart about doing what's best.

Even if you feel that a part of your life as you knew it, or dreamed it, is over, another part of your life is beginning. You are going to be in transition for a while, from here to where you want to be. The decisions you make in the process of becoming unmarried will affect how you and your family make a new start. To make a new beginning, it helps to first make a good ending.

Getting the right expert advice about the many things that can go wrong *and* right in your legal and financial decision making can help you in the process. That is the first step on your way to **taking charge of your future**.

There's a saying: "It takes a village to raise a child." Many of us who have been down the road of ending a marriage can tell you that it takes a village of professionals, friends, family, neighbors, colleagues, and wise counselors—co-travelers who can help you find your way and have been through the messy, scary, sad, confusing, and sometimes hopeful process of untying the knots.

It's said that we cannot go back and change the past. What we can do is make sure the past doesn't keep us from having a better future. Today you can begin with a smart start down that road — by finding someone you trust who has the experience to help you navigate, one step at a time, the emotional and legal labyrinth of becoming unmarried.

—Nance Guilmartin, author of *Healing Conversations: What to Say When You Don't Know What to Say*, and *The Power of Pause: How to Be More Effective in a Demanding 24/7 World*. More about Nance at www.nanceguilmartin. com

REMEMBER THAT THIS SHORT GUIDE IS NOT A SUBSTITUTE FOR LEGAL ADVICE FROM AN ASTUTE LAWYER FAMILIAR WITH YOUR SITUATION. IN FACT, THERE IS NO SUBSTITUTE FOR LEGAL ADVICE FROM A THOUGHTFUL LAWYER FAMILIAR WITH YOUR SITUATION. YOUR RECEIPT OF THIS BOOK IN ANY FORM DOESN'T MAKE YOU MY CLIENT OR ME YOUR ATTORNEY. WHEN CLIENTS UNDERSTAND THE TOPICS IN THIS BOOKLET, I FIND THEY HAVE A BETTER CHANCE FOR SUCCESS. I ALSO FIND THEY ARE ABLE TO ENDURE THE DIVORCE PROCESS WITH LESS STRESS. THIS BOOK IS WRITTEN BY A CALIFORNIA LAWYER ABOUT DIVORCE IN CALIFORNIA ONLY.

INTRODUCTION

I'm Facing Divorce; Where Do I Start?

Right now you may feel like you've lost control of your life, like everything is uncertain. You undoubtedly have so many questions that you don't know where to start. This guide is a great place to begin because what you don't know *can* hurt you, and what you learn can *help* you.

> *Should I just leave?*
> *Can I make my spouse get out?*
> *What about money? What about debts?*
> *Who's going to get the house? The property?*
> *What about the children? Will they be protected?*
> *Is it possible to have a good divorce?*

Is there such thing as a good divorce? I'd like to think so. Even divorces that can't be made *good* can be made *better*. The people who enjoy the greatest sense of success in a divorce are those who can bring themselves to compromise. Compromise can be difficult, especially when there seems to be clear right and wrong. It requires thoughtfulness, conscious effort, and logic in the midst of what feels like a completely *illogical* experience. Having a *better* divorce, and not the urban guerrilla-warfare divorce, requires being self-aware and telling apart those battles which *must* be fought from those which *may* be fought.

When making a decision in my own life, I ask myself this question: **"Will this matter to me in six months? Next year? Five years from now?"** If the result of a decision is something I won't care about after a year, the decision probably isn't that important. Today, at the very beginning of your information-gathering mission, is the day to think about the decisions you'll be making soon.

> *Six months from now, or after your court case is over, what do you hope your life will look like? If you can look further ahead than six months, do it. It is this vision of your future—not that of tomorrow or next week—that must drive your decision-making process.*

This eye-opening guide is designed to answer some of your questions, explain the basics of the divorce process, and give you practical advice about helping yourself and moving forward in your life. The process isn't going to be easy. You may feel angry, and you probably feel hurt. For most, that gets better with time, but not usually as a direct result of the legal process. It's important not to expect family court to be therapeutic. While the process can bring closure and certainty, few look back on their divorce as a pleasant experience. Take heart, though. It can at least be made *less* unpleasant. This guide is offered to educate and empower you. A happy, satisfying future for you and your children depends on you getting good information and preparation, which lead to realistic expectations.

1

NO-FAULT DIVORCE:
IS THERE SUCH A THING?

Whose Fault Is This Mess Anyway?

No legal matter I come across is shrouded in more misinformation than no-fault divorce. It's natural when you're getting a divorce to want to blame someone. It makes perfect sense emotionally. I have seen people expend much emotional energy trying to identify or sometimes *create* fault. In a no-fault state like California, those efforts are misdirected. Does that mean there is no fault, ever? No. Sometimes there definitely is fault. *No-fault* just means the law doesn't always see your situation in the same way you or your spouse might.

California is a no-fault-divorce state. This means that *in California*, if you want a divorce, you can get one without having to prove that your spouse has done something wrong. Of course, this also means that if your spouse wants a divorce, there's really no way to prevent it from happening, even though you yourself may have done nothing wrong.

> *Under current California no-fault divorce law, the only legal ground necessary for divorce is the existence of* **irreconcilable differences.**

Irreconcilable differences is a term that really means one of you no longer wants to be with the other. Irreconcilable differences is a state of mind understood only by the divorcee, so **the only proof needed of irreconcilable differences is for one spouse to say they exist.** If one of you says that you have irreconcilable differences, the claim cannot be legally disputed.

Why Do We Have No-Fault Divorce?

A generation or so ago, California eliminated the old law of fault-based divorce. "Fault" law would only allow you to get a divorce if you could prove that your spouse had cheated on you, had abandoned you, or was guilty of extreme cruelty to you or your children. You also had to be fault-free yourself.

Prior to the change in law, many people found themselves stuck in unwanted marriages. They couldn't prove fault, which would have allowed them to get a divorce. In those days, not getting along wasn't enough. Not even what today would be considered extreme mental or emotional abuse qualified a suffering spouse for divorce.

The coming of no-fault divorce law has helped eliminate these problems. No one is legally forced to remain in a broken marriage just because there is no good proof of fault. Likewise, no longer can one spouse gain a legal advantage in family court by accusing the other of having an affair or abandoning the marriage.

How Does No-Fault Divorce Work?

How does no-fault law affect my divorce case?

Can I tell the judge what my spouse did wrong?
Can my spouse stop me from getting a divorce?
Can I prevent my cheating spouse from having access to our children?

For starters, no-fault law provides that even though you may be outraged by what you view as your spouse's shocking, disgraceful, appallingly indecent or deceitful behavior, **you may never get to mention a word about it in family court**. It also means that if you want to leave a marriage for reasons your spouse disagrees with (say, irreconcilable differences?), he or she cannot use any fault of your own to stop you from getting a divorce.

What you can expect is not always what you think, even when you're certain of what you deserve.

When considering granting a divorce, a California family court judge doesn't want to hear that a husband was a serial adulterer or that a wife took the children and ran off to move in with her boyfriend before the divorce was final. Fault plays no part in a spouse's right to end the marital relationship. The absence of misbehavior from divorce court discussion can be frustrating for those who expect an opportunity to vent their anger and (sometimes quite justified) frustration.

Don't expect family court to be an open forum where your grievances against one another are aired.

If you need help coping with the stress of your situation, a good private counselor can provide more relief and practical help than a family court judge or attorney could. In a divorce where child custody is at issue, parenting ability may be discussed. Fault has no impact on this discussion either, unless the bad behavior has a particular effect on the children. Examples include criminal activity directed at or engaged in, in the presence of the children, lewd behavior, drug or alcohol abuse and, of course, child abuse or domestic violence. One parent may have trouble with the idea that the court may consider a former spouse who commits adultery or loses his or her 401(k) at the gaming tables to nevertheless be a suitable co-parent.

In court, judges sometimes say: "While the parents may no longer be right for one another as husband and wife, they're divorcing each other, not the children."

Does Fault Ever Matter When Ending a Marriage?

On some very specific issues, facts showing fault can still be relevant. Their relevance, though, goes not to the ending of the marriage but to the judge's orders about custody and visitation. This guide will explain these situations in more detail later, so keep reading to learn how a spouse's behaving badly can affect the outcome of a case.

2

THE DIVORCE PROCESS

The Beginning: Filing for Divorce
It's All About Paperwork and Timing

A bout every six months, like clockwork, I get a call from someone—say, a new bride-to-be—who is about to get remarried. She is in a panic. She went to get a new marriage license to remarry, only to discover she is still married to her first husband. It is always the same story: she either didn't file the divorce paperwork correctly or was depending on someone else to file it for her. She is unpleasantly surprised to find she is not really divorced.

The process for filing for a divorce in California begins when you and/or your divorce attorney draft a *petition*, a document that provides the court with basic information about you, your spouse, and your children. It also states the *relief* you, the *petitioner*, are requesting, those provisions you think you will need to move on from the marriage. Put another way, relief is what you want out of the divorce. You may request in the petition as much or as little as you prefer—within the limits of California divorce law. In other words, it's okay for your Petition to contain *more* detail than the form requires, but it's not okay for it to contain *less* detail than the minimum required.

The petition is then **filed** with the court, and once your spouse has been **served** with the petition, along with a **summons** and other **mandatory documents**, the family court case is officially underway.

Okay, I filed and had my spouse served. What happens next?

After you file and have your Summons, Petition, etc. served, your soon-to-be ex-spouse has three options of response.

1. **Uncontested:** You file a petition; your spouse files a timely response (within thirty days of being served). The parties enter into an agreement. Forms are completed and exchanged; some are filed with the court. If all goes as planned, a judgment of dissolution is entered, part of which is the agreement. Six months after the court "obtains jurisdiction over the respondent," **married status** (legally recognized marriage) is ended.

2. **Default:** You file a petition, and your spouse is served with it and a summons. Your spouse files no response within thirty days of being served. You request right away that default be entered. Depending on how much property is involved in the case, the court may have a *default prove-up* hearing to make sure all mandatory forms are filed and all mandatory procedures complied with. Judgment is entered, and six months after the court obtains jurisdiction over the respondent, married status ends.

3. *Contested:* You file a petition, and your spouse is served with it and a summons. Either party may then file an **order to show cause** for pretrial orders, usually on issues of child support, spousal support, custody, or visitation. If there is a custody or visitation dispute, an FCS (Family Court Services) mediation is performed, and a hearing on the issues is held. The judge makes *temporary orders*, which often become permanent.

The two timelines for your divorce. Once your spouse is served with the summons, petition, and other papers, a **thirty-day clock** begins ticking off the time during which he or she—the **respondent** if you filed the petition—can file a written **response**. The response can state facts, ask for relief (child support, spousal support, etc.), and defend against claims you've made in your petition. A **six-month clock**—showing the countdown to the earliest date your official singlehood may begin—begins to tick when the respondent is served with the summons and other papers.

What Information **Must** *I Provide at the Time of Filing for Divorce?*

Every California divorce petition must contain certain information. First we will look at what's required in the petition. Then we will look at other documents you must file with the court.

The petition must state:

- That at the time of filing, at least one of you **has lived long enough—six months—in the state of California** for a California court to have *jurisdiction* (the legal power of a court to hear and decide a case).

- That at the time of filing, at least one of the parties has lived long enough—three months—in the county where the case is filed.

- All *minor children* of the relationship. Each child's name, age, and date of birth must appear. **Children born to a couple *during* marriage are *presumed* under the law to be children *of* the marriage. Children born to a couple *before* marriage must be first *determined to be children of the marriage* before the court can make orders regarding custody, visitation, or support of those children. Check the correct box if you have children born before marriage.**

- The *relief* you are requesting. *Relief* is sort of like *result*. You can ask for child custody, child support, spousal support, return of separate property, division of community property, and assignment of separate and community debts.

In addition, the petitioner must complete a *summons* (the form that tells the respondent he or she is being sued and other actions are being taken) and, where children are involved, a *Declaration Under the Uniform Child Custody Jurisdiction and Enforcement Act*. Some *local court forms* are often required at the beginning of the case. These differ from one county to the next.

The Ins and Outs of Filing

The Petition, Summons and other initial forms must be filed, and the proper fees must be paid, in the correct *court clerk's office*—that is, the business office of the correct court (the court in the *county where you live*). For directions about deciding which court is the right one for your divorce case, take a look at the *county court website* of your county of residence. Use any search portal (Google, Bing, Yahoo!, etc.). Input your keywords like so: "San Diego County Superior Court." Hit Enter. That should get you on your way to the site you need.

The *initial filing fee* is a constantly changing figure, When I started writing this, it was $395.00. As I put in the final edits, it's up to $435.00. In addition, the court may require you to pay *other fees* (for filing motions in the case and often for court reporters).

Once the respondent (your soon-to-be ex-spouse) has had the Summons and other initial papers for at least thirty days and has not responded, you, the petitioner, may request a default judgment. If the Respondent filed a Response,, the case goes forward with contested issues.

When Is the Six-Month Waiting Period Not Really Six Months?

One day, you overhear your coworker (who is extremely savvy with Internet research) handing out water cooler divorce advice to an office manager from another department. The question of the day is, **Are you automatically divorced after six months?** The response is, **Oh yeah, you're automatically divorced six months after your case is filed. I know because my brother-in-law's second cousin told him.**

NOOOOOoooooo! Many people entering the California divorce process have heard of the so-called *six month rule*, a waiting period designed to give divorcing couples a chance to cool off, consider their options, seek needed counseling and decide whether divorce is really what they want.

Many people mistakenly take this mandatory waiting period to mean that the entire divorce process lasts six months. It does not. What the rule actually provides is this:

> **In California, the *earliest* date on which married status can be terminated is six months from the date the court *acquires jurisdiction* over the *respondent*.**

Great! you say. More legalese! What on earth does *acquires jurisdiction* mean? **As you are introduced to some of the forms you'll be seeing, bear with me as I explain the new vocabulary.** The court acquires jurisdiction when:

- the respondent is *served* with the *Summons and Petition* (the court papers filed by you, the petitioner); or
- the respondent, without having been served the Summons and Petition, discovers a case has been started and files a Response.

All of this means the respondent has been notified that the court case that will end the marriage has begun. The respondent can defend (fight back), and the court now has jurisdiction (power) to make orders that affect the respondent.

So the six-month waiting period begins…
> **But…**
> **Your married status is *not* automatically terminated six months from the beginning of the case. Not six months after the filing, not six months after the respondent is served, *not automatically, ever.***

So When Will I Really Be Single?

In reality, the length of the court process usually has little to do with the date the case was begun or the expiration of the six-month waiting period. The divorce process in California involves the resolution of several legal issues, and termination of your married status is only one of them.

On the other hand, family court departments have the flexibility to sort through issues in a sequence that makes sense for your individual case. Certainly, if there's good reason, and your six-month waiting period has elapsed, your divorce attorney can file the necessary papers asking the family court to order the termination of your married status; this process is called *bifurcation*.

In fact, ***the law allows your family court judge to order the termination of your married status at any of these points in your divorce***:

- *At the time of* decision of your other issues, such as property division, child custody, visitation, and support. (This is the most common instance.)
- When either spouse files a motion requesting *bifurcation*—a separate order granting termination of your married status made ***before*** other issues are addressed. (This could be desirable, for example, if you or your spouse is ready to remarry.)
- ***After*** other issues have been determined. (Occasionally, couples agree to this *delay* in the termination of married status for tax, health insurance or religious purposes.)

Often people are okay with waiting for termination of married status in order to finish everything at once. It's usually less costly and more efficient to do it all at the same time. However, depending on the extent to which you and your spouse are able to agree, the process to fully resolve a divorce case easily ***can*** and usually ***does*** take longer than six months.

3

DIVORCE: IN THE COURTS?
MEDIATION? OR...?

Litigation, Arbitration,
Mediation or Collaboration

L et's face it: if you're going to get divorced, you're going to need to choose how to proceed. Should you
seek litigation? Mediation? Does divorce collaboration
work in your particular situation? Being involved in any
kind of court proceeding means (gulp) getting acquainted
with some jargon. I will explain some of the pros and cons
of each process along the way. *Let's get started*.

Litigation: Generally, litigation, an adversarial process, leaves all final decisions to the judge rather than the
parties. A case may offer the opportunity to litigate a lot,
a little, or not at all. People find that litigation can be difficult and is always confrontational. But it can be the best
way to get the job done.

If you must litigate, do it strategically. Generally
speaking, it is easier to accomplish what you want by the
use of *motions* or participation in *order-to-show-cause*
(lately renamed "Request for Order") hearings. These
are usually less formal than trials, but not necessarily so.

People are encouraged to negotiate, fewer witnesses are called (sometimes none), and the paperwork leading up to the hearing is less tedious. There's also usually much less paperwork. That means you save money, time, and headaches. Leave only the most challenging issues for a trial.

You know your spouse better than anyone. If you know that your spouse isn't going to compromise on *anything*, don't feel obligated to waste time and money exploring alternatives to litigation. Too often, I have seen one spouse object to a proposal only because it was the other spouse's idea. An unreasonable spouse may leave you no alternative but to litigate. If you are going to need extensive litigation, let your attorney take on all the drama your contentious spouse wants to create—it can be a big relief. Bite the bullet and get through it.

Arbitration: Pretty much identical to litigation, but instead of a court judge, the contestants use an ***arbitrator*** whom they agree upon. For the most part, the same rules apply. If it's so much like litigation, why use it? You might ask. Privacy, mostly. Court records are public. People who wish to keep their laundry—dirty or not—private can do so by using arbitration. Arbitration is a quasi-judicial process conducted outside the court. It ends in an arbitration award which must then be "confirmed" as a judgment.

Mediation: The opposite of the two you just read. Mediation can be very structured, but usually it's not. It's typically an informal process, in a less formal setting (than a courtroom). Mediation is often presented by its proponents as a way to minimize both conflict and attorney's fees in a case. I'm not convinced it always accomplishes those aims, but that doesn't mean it isn't sometimes the best vehicle to use.

In mediation, there may not even be any insistence on following the law. Unequal divisions of property and unconventional child-sharing plans are often acceptable. However, in mediation, each party needs to know *what the law, if invoked, would provide* so that each party can make informed decisions. Don't be put off by what may seem a touchy-feely approach to problem solving in your divorce. There will be a considerable amount of compromise and negotiation. However, the informal nature of mediation leads to each party feeling they've been heard out, and for some, that's every bit as important as the tangible substance of the case.

Let's assume that you have decided on mediation, but before you did so, you and your spouse tried to negotiate your divorce at your kitchen table. Any couple would have had a hard time with this conversation without help—and there's already plenty of tension in the relationship. A good lawyer, or two, can make the process more manageable. An attorney focusing on a mediated divorce won't represent either of you, will remain impartial and will instead work toward a negotiated solution for the two of you.

Couples interested in mediation usually have one priority above all others: *Let's not get into a fight.* The primary benefit of mediation is that both of you receive solid legal advice on which to base your decisions without having to resort to litigation. This does not mean that the mediating family lawyer gives you the "right" answers; rather he or she will tell you everything you need to know, including the long-term ramifications of your decisions. It is up to you to decide what solutions fit. Spouses who are engaged in the mediation process often choose to also confer with their own attorneys, independently. If the main disagreement is about child custody and visitation, the skills of a mental health professional will be more useful.

Word of warning: Mediation isn't the answer for everyone. Mediation doesn't work well when one spouse is much more dominant in the relationship, when one spouse just won't compromise, and when there's a big difference between spouses in education, earning ability, sophistication or language skills.

Collaboration: A relatively recent concept, the collaborative process involves enlisting a handful of experts and entrusting them to come up with a menu of workable solutions. For example, a psychologist is brought in to analyze child custody matters, an accountant is brought in to analyze tax implications, a financial planner is brought in to negotiate property division, and so on. No member of this panel may later represent either spouse if the parties are unable to reach collaborative resolution.

Collaborative divorce is a brand of *alternative dispute resolution* (ADR for short), in addition to arbitration and mediation. It's great for people who (a) really, *really* want to get along, (b) have been doing pretty well at it already, and (c) are terrified (or maybe just really worried) about unleashing their lawyers to litigate.

I'm a big fan of the collaborative process, and have worked with collaborative attorneys to resolve some cases. Collaboration gives clients a fuller range of expert information. It is especially beneficial for business owners whose divorces may be complicated by their financial pictures. Regrettably, it can be cost prohibitive because each spouse must pay not only his or her own attorney but also the experts. The parties may avoid conflict, but will spend a considerable sum of money doing so.

Whether you decide on litigation, arbitration, mediation, or collaboration, it's critical to get good advice so you understand the implications of your decisions for today, five years from now, and a lifetime.

4

GOING NAKED: WHO NEEDS A LAWYER ANYWAY?

You may be thinking, *These are the days of do-it-yourself. Hey, why would I want to spend a bunch of money on attorney's fees? After all, you just have to fill out the forms, right?*

Um…no.

In my practice I get calls every day from people who chose not to use a lawyer, even in cases involving homes, children, pension plans, or all of the above and more. They have since discovered that some part of the court proceedings requires extensive (and expensive) damage control. The damage could easily have been avoided with legal advice, and they may have discovered that the damage *cannot be undone or controlled*! The client's approach, the result of decisions based on good intentions, has backfired because he didn't fully understand his actions' legal implications.

A negotiated resolution needs to be based on informed decisions, and the process does not have to be costly or marked by hostility. An attorney doesn't have to do everything, but good advice will cost you less than the potential financial and emotional price of "going naked."

Here are some real-life examples of the results of passing up good legal advice:

- The spouses agree one will get more property while the other will not have to pay child support. The problem? An agreement to waive child support is unenforceable. In fact it's *void*!

- The spouses, who live in different states, agree that once their three-year-old reaches school age, she will spend one year with one parent, the next with the other. Their reasoning? This is "fair to each parent." When this agreement gets to court—as all such agreements inevitably seem to—the agreement fails to hold water. It eventually dawns on one parent or both that the arrangement is too disruptive for the child. Just because the arrangement was "agreed to" in the form of a contract doesn't mean a judge won't tell both parents it isn't in the child's best interests.

- The spouses agree to divide their property equally, but they make serious mistakes trying to figure out what's community (each gets half) property and what's not. This is particularly tricky with pensions and retirement funds. No one wants to be old and broke. Even experienced, well-trained lawyers sometimes disagree on how much of whose retirement money should be split equally, so it's never surprising when nonlawyers get it wrong.

- The spouses agree that some relative (usually a grandparent) can exercise a parent's time with a child. Sometimes this results from a genuine desire by one parent, and sometimes it's insisted on by an absent parent in order to preserve his "time share" so child support doesn't change. Problem? Yes. Nonparent rights are tricky and not nearly as absolute as those of parents. Parents have certain generalized rights and responsibilities which exist even in the absence of a court order. For example: the right to associate with the children, the duty to protect and support them. For nonparents, those rights must be created by a court order.

- The spouses agree to a division of property that is so lopsided as to be outrageous by any definition other than that of the spouse who gains the advantage. This usually results from either a domestic violence victim's agreement to unconscionable terms just to get out of a relationship or a sophisticated spouse's exploitation of the other's lack of legal savvy.

Waiting too long to start damage control. In each of the last three scenarios, there are time limits within which one must go to court and ask a judge to fix the big mistake(s). Most of these time limits are set in stone, so getting a do-over after the last bell has rung isn't going to happen. If you wait too long to act, it won't matter how unfair the result of your negotiation was; the court won't be able to help. Which deadline applies? They range from ten days to two years. Don't guess. Get professional advice.

Nowhere outside of divorce negotiations is it more true that *an ounce of prevention is worth a pound of cure.* This is one important reason to have a legal guide help you understand how to get the best result possible in your particular situation.

5

HIRING A LAWYER: MAKE SURE YOU KNOW WHAT YOU'RE GETTING

Many people only think of hiring a lawyer after things have blown up. Though they've watched enough TV to know legal ignorance can leave them at a disadvantage in a courtroom situation, they figure unless—or until—things get out of control, they'll enjoy not having to pay an attorney. In reality, the greatest need for and value of legal advice and representation is in making sure their time in the courtroom is minimized or avoided altogether. *The best lawyers know most problems are best resolved outside the courtroom!*

Unfortunately, many people don't consider hiring a family law attorney until it's too late. They don't understand the value of a good attorney or are afraid they'll be taken advantage of by an attorney. It seems everyone has a shocking story to tell that involves a family law attorney. These stories will curl your hair. Sadly, some of them are true.

To make sure you hire the right person, you must interview your prospective attorney! Many of the awful vignettes we hear from friends, family and coworkers are the result of communication problems. Many of these communication problems could have been avoided had the right questions been asked during the attorney interview. Lawyer and client should be able to be *direct* with one another. If you're uneasy with your lawyer, you may be poorly matched. Conversations about case strategy should always include you. At every step of the court process, your lawyer should be educating and involving you. So before you sign on the dotted line, be sure that the attorney you're interviewing sees you as an important player on the team. Go ahead. **Ask your toughest questions**.

If I were ending a marriage, these are some questions I would ask in my first interview with a family law attorney:

- *Is what I want realistic?*
- *How long will this take?*
- *What things* **affect** *how long this will take?*
- *How much is this going to cost—in the best case? And if things don't go as expected?*
- *Do you have an alternative method of compensation to the traditional "billable hour"? (Ask about fixed fees, which limit your risk of an unmanageably high bill and may also limit the extent of the attorney's work.)*
- *In the interest of keeping the level of conflict to a minimum, do you see yourself collaborating with me and the other side to get to a result we can all live with?*
- *What role do you expect clients to play in a case?*
- *How do you handle it when clients disagree with your advice?*

Asking these questions of an attorney can be uncomfortable, but a little clarity in the beginning can save you stress later.

Find out about your lawyer's philosophy of practice during the first meeting.

Family Lawyers Who Bill Hourly

Now, for a small bit of editorializing. Until just a few years ago, for sixteen years, I billed hourly, just like my mentors and colleagues. Clients would come see me, I would ask for a retainer of, say, $1500-$7500, and the retainer would be used up on work done on their case. So, I would send a bill to cover the work not paid for by the retainer. Clients, who were already under both economic and emotional stress weren't ready to get a bill. *We had a problem.*

I knew in the back of my mind that something wasn't working in this situation. I just wasn't sure what needed to be fixed. One day I had to ask myself, "Would I, if I needed a lawyer for a divorce, sign a blank check over to another attorney?" The answer turned out to be, "Nope, probably not." So, how could I expect other people to do the very thing I was reluctant to do myself? **Thus, I abandoned the billable-hour model**. I changed to a fixed-fee method. So far, everybody is happier. Read on to find out why.

Fixed-fee billing means the attorney and client agree on a certain amount of money for certain services. Yes, the operative word here is *certain*. No ugly surprises at the end of this month or next, or any month, for that matter.

It's a refreshing approach that offers the client the security of knowing what his risk is. It is nicer for the client not to be thinking while he's on the phone with me, "Oh my God! The meter's running!" While I like to think I was always conscientious enough to work efficiently for my clients when using the billable-hour model, fixed fees offer the attorney an additional incentive to be efficient and to not over-litigate a case.

This approach to pricing and paying for legal services is liberating for both client and attorney. The attorney gets to focus on solving the client's problems instead of slavishly recording and billing for each task the attorney performs. The client gets the comfort of knowing no dreaded billable-hour statement is coming in the mail. Most family law clients have a limited legal services budget; most do not have the resources to write a check for a few - or several - thousand dollars in a given month. Who needs the stress?

So, this is how I do it. Fixed fees at least let clients know what financial cost to expect.

6

WHAT'S YOUR STORY? TALKING TO YOUR LAWYER

Deceive not thy physician, confessor, nor lawyer.
George Herbert

What can you do to help make everything clear for your lawyer?

These days I frequently have clients with drug problems seeking divorce. They swear to me they are clean, but then opposing counsel requests a drug test. When the test comes back dirty, the client's case is hurt. *Tell your attorney the absolute truth*—even about the things you might not want to tell anybody. It is extremely important for your lawyer to know both the strengths and the weaknesses of your case.

If child custody is in dispute, have you been the primary care giving parent? If child support is in dispute, can you prove your estranged spouse is claiming a lower-than-actual income? Tell your attorney what you know and how it can be proven. The catch there is that you've likely signed off on joint tax returns. Where those returns have understated income, you've participated – maybe even unknowingly – in making the spouse's defense for him / her. Oops. That will hurt your case.

Why is it important for your lawyer to know everything—even things you'd rather not talk about? It allows your attorney to plan a solution for you if you are confronted by the other side with mistakes you have made. Let's say you used to drink too much, maybe even have a DUI or two. But you're sober now, have been for a while. Your lawyer will need to know how long you've been sober, whether you're in AA, and, if so, who your sponsor is. She might also ask if you're willing to take a drug test. All this will enable her to hit back at allegations that you're going to endanger the children by driving drunk.

Sometimes a client believes what she has done is so wrong, shameful or embarrassing she couldn't hope to overcome the effects of it. She stays silent about it and, instead of confiding in her lawyer, loses sleep over it. If she would only speak up with her lawyer, he could tell his client her fears are unfounded. The client has needlessly worried about something a court might readily overlook. On a few occasions, I've had clients who had an affair or started a new relationship before the divorce was final, and were suffering under the mistaken belief that their behavior would disqualify them from having custody of the children. Some had even been prepared to give up primary custody of the children!

The Internet and your divorce.

Tell your attorney even those things you believe your spouse doesn't know. Your ex-to-be just might know more than you think! Remember that the lawyer on the other side may have a number of very enterprising methods for finding information to use against you. There are databases these days with very personal information. Because of the Internet, it is hard to keep a secret. E-mails, Facebook, blog posts, and tweets are gold mines for the imaginative attorney (and for the angry ex-to-be!). Don't let your attorney be surprised by secret information revealed at some crucial point in your case, like during mediation or at trial. Surprises make your attorney unprepared to defend you, and that does not translate into a good result for you. While we're on the subject of the Internet, make *absolutely certain* that you have changed and secured all your passwords and user names before initiating your divorce.

Telling your *whole story* to your attorney is important, even if you're not litigating and you're confident you'll never be testifying under oath. *Concealing information can undercut your cause even in the negotiation process.* **Just because you won't be taking the stand doesn't mean it isn't important to be honest with your attorney. It's vital. Always.**

Help document your case! Spend some time gathering documentation and making written notes about your situation, including dates and details. Your lawyer will be not only grateful but more effective. For example, if you've been the Lone Ranger as a parent, shouldering pretty much all the responsibility, but the other parent claims to have shared equally in the parenting, it will be helpful to show school records reflecting you've been at the parent-teacher conferences—alone. If you are alleging your spouse has perpetrated domestic violence against you, or if you are *accused of domestic violence,* you'll want to provide your attorney with the names and contact information of known *witnesses* to avoid a he-said-she-said scenario.

Be prepared to brainstorm with your attorney and his staff about your situation! The attorney's staff is bound by the same duty of confidentiality as the attorney himself. The most successful clients I know are the ones who took time to 1) help their lawyers think through what was most important to them, the clients, and 2) explain what they believed to be the best way to pursue their goals.

Don't assume just because you're not the expert that your ideas aren't valuable and valid. I've gotten some brilliant ideas from clients. In one case my client moved five doors down from the other parent, who stayed in the original home. There was a subsequent dispute about child custody. The other parent argued the child should live primarily in the home most familiar to her. In a genius statement of the obvious, my client came up with this: "Houses don't raise children. Parents do." At the end of a lengthy oral argument, that was the phrase I closed with. It succinctly summarized our entire argument. We won.

Respect deadlines! Being on time can make or break your case. Not getting things in on time will cost you money and stress. To illustrate just a couple of examples among many court deadlines, consider these: The date a motion requesting support is *filed* has a profound effect on the date the order can be made *effective*. If you're *opposing* a motion, you must have your opposition filed and served by a set deadline. Missing the date can mean your evidence won't be considered by the judge, or that the hearing will be delayed. If you are confused by something, call your attorney and get an answer to your question. When you're not clear on what your attorney wants, just ask. Your attorney may assume you understand her instructions. Don't be embarrassed to say, "Can you please explain this? I'm still unclear." When things don't get done on time, your lawyer experiences delays in getting your case finished. **Deadlines have no mercy.** Instead of allowing yourself to feel helpless and overwhelmed, empower yourself by helping gather documentation needed to support your legal claims. In the days, weeks or even months leading up to any court appearance, you will need to furnish the Court and your opponent documents which either *are* the evidence you intend to submit, or describe that evidence. If you're late getting these things turned in, the other side will object to your evidence being considered.

7

MOVING TOWARD RESOLUTION: MARITAL SETTLEMENT AGREEMENT— THE END IS IN SIGHT!

If the phrase *marital settlement agreement* (MSA) comes up in your attorney's vocabulary as a way to conclude your case, it means you haven't gone to trial to have a judge decide the issues. It usually means the end is in sight and it looks like you'll be able to make a deal with your spouse. It is almost always a good thing.

The vast majority of cases—about 95 percent—are resolved using marital settlement agreements, while the remaining few go to trial.[1] In California family court, reasonableness during the negotiation process is so highly regarded that a judge can impose penalties—*sanctions*—for stubbornness or bullying.

Professional guidance is a must in all but the simplest cases. Just because marital settlement agreements are common, don't think they're not complicated. An

---

[1] 95% is an unofficial estimate of cases that resolve without trial shared by myself and many other practitioners who have written on the topic. Also see: CBSNEWS.COM FOR FEB. 11, 2009. Apparently, www.courts.ca.gov, the California Courts' official site, regrettably doesn't provide this data in its report.

MSA is a document that explains exactly what agreements between you and your spouse are with regard to child custody, visitation, and support, and how property, debt and retirement benefits will be divided. Just to be clear, remember that pretty much anything you can think of that might be argued about in a divorce case is discussed in detail in the MSA. The document needs to be done right. It needs to be done in a way that is valid, is enforceable, and accomplishes your goals.

These days, it seems like more and more people are mistaking their situation for one of those "simplest cases." Don't be lulled into complacency when your case lacks the fireworks of domestic violence, abuse, rampant legal motions in court, or mudslinging. Just because emotions aren't volcanic doesn't mean the stakes aren't high.

I once had a client who quietly agreed in writing to let her husband keep a marital estate *he* said was worth half a million dollars. She got debt - and *only* debt - out of the deal. The deal was done and filed with the court months before I met with the client for the first time. I was able to unwind the judgment, alleging duress, undue influence, and excusable mistake, and the judge was prepared to find that the husband had committed fraud. But if the client had missed the deadline for the motion we filed, she could easily have been out of luck, even though the husband had behaved very badly indeed. It was a very close call on the timing. Vigilance is needed even when the level of conflict feels pretty low.

Agree for the right reasons with excellent advice. The right reasons? Here are just a few: You've gotten good advice. You and your spouse know that on most issues the result of agreement would be similar to that of court appearance, and you want to save the costs of litigation. On controversial issues, you and your spouse have been able to negotiate—again, with good advice—an informal deal.

The wrong reasons? Avoiding conflict at all costs, bullying from the other side, and fear that going to court is risky, expensive and unpredictable. Excellent legal advice will help take your fear down a notch, or several, even when you've been the victim of domestic violence, or you've assumed that because you've *perpetrated* domestic violence, you've lost all rights as a parent.

Don't think of settlement as an all-or-nothing proposition. Sometimes, a couple can agree on many things, just not *everything*. For them to have come so far and then throw up their hands in frustration and head for trial on *all* issues wouldn't make sense. Rather than wasting the progress they've made, they should put into writing what they *have* resolved and present to the judge only those issues on which they have reached an impasse.

There are several benefits to seeking wise legal advice early in your divorce process in order to reach a voluntary agreement that finishes your case. The benefits include:

- Your divorce will be *over faster*, with minimal court involvement.
- You will avoid an ongoing dispute and thereby *reduce stress on both you and your children*. It's

easy to underestimate just how perceptive children are about what's going on, even when parents are silent.

- You'll *save the expenses* of litigation and trial, including additional attorney's fees, expert witnesses' fees (those of accountants, psychologists, et al.), and court costs.

- *You can get things that the judge can't give you!* **At trial** a family court judge decides what the facts are and then is limited to ruling according to sometimes very narrow statutory rights guaranteed by California divorce law. On the other hand the decision to carefully craft an MSA, a contract *that becomes a court order*, means the parties can tailor a set of agreements and arrangements that truly suits their needs in ways the law could not on its own. In other words, an MSA can afford the parties the opportunity to contract for benefits that would not be available to them through simply submitting their case for rulings by a family court judge.

Here are just a few examples of arrangements that can be made by agreement:

If yours has been a *long-duration marriage* (ten years or longer), you may be entitled to *indefinite spousal support*, sometimes called *alimony* or *spousal maintenance*. Don't give up such a benefit without serious thought and good advice. The court cannot put a stop on its own power to award spousal support. However, if there are other, more important things you want out of the divorce, *you, who would otherwise seek such support, can use it as a bargaining chip*. Agreeing to receipt of a discounted amount of spousal support and even waiving family court's jurisdiction, or power, to order spousal support are doable in a marital settlement agreement, but would be impossible for a judge.

The court must set *child support* according to state *child support guidelines*, and there's little or no room for deviation. With a settlement agreement, however, *you can agree to an amount of child support that is higher or lower* than the guideline amount. Exercise great caution, though. Special rules come into play on a non-guideline order.

How and When Are Marital Settlement Agreements Enforced?

An MSA is usually *merged* into a final judgment. In other words, the terms of your settlement agreement will become part of the final court order in your case. As a result, your settlement agreement can be enforced in exactly the same ways as any other court order, and failure by a party to abide by its terms can be considered contempt of court.

It is important that your MSA be carefully drafted. For this reason, you should have an attorney who practices California family law at least look yours over before it is filed—*especially* if you've chosen to divorce without otherwise using a lawyer.

Remember that even though your MSA is a contract that becomes an order, the rules for interpreting and enforcing it are not always traditional **contract law.** *When provisions of the Family Code conflict with traditional contract laws contained in any other Code or even in published appeals cases, Family Code trumps!*

If your settlement agreement is *not written properly, it can be found to be unenforceable in court.*

Over the years I have unwound or invalidated a number of MSAs containing provisions that not only went beyond what the law would default to, but went beyond what the law would *tolerate*. In other words, while your settlement agreement can give you more than what a black-letter-law-bound family court judge can, it cannot give you rights which *violate* the law. I have seen people try to agree that *neither party will ever be required to pay child support*. **Likewise, proposals that one parent terminate his parental rights in exchange for relief from paying child support are void.** These are perfect examples of unenforceable provisions; They violate public policy ensuring support of children. It is the policy of the state of California that each parent shoulders his / her duty to financially support the children. [California Family Code Section 3600 *et seq.*]

While an MSA is an effective tool for resolving disputes between parties, it should be crafted with great care.

How can I make a mistake with an MSA? Don't judges spot mistakes? Judges don't typically review MSAs. *No one in the court system has a responsibility to make sure that an MSA submitted for filing passes muster for fairness, enforceability or even good grammar.* Once a judgment is handed to a clerk for processing, it isn't edited by court staff. Awful errors can go unseen until months or years later, when the judgment actually *is* read by a judge or an attorney. The occasion is usually marked by a party's court motion to enforce or invalidate the judgment. Damage control isn't always possible. When undoing (vacating) a judgment *is* possible, the process is ugly and expensive, and the need for it is tragically and completely preventable.

8

CUSTODY MEDIATION AND FAMILY COURT

The Rule to Remember: Avoid a Meltdown

If you're involved in a child custody or visitation dispute in family court in the state of California, you will be meeting in *Family Court Services mediation* with a court-appointed counselor (formerly called "mediator"); that is, unless you're one of the fortunate who can afford a private mediator. Those who do private mediation can bypass Family Court Services. In either event, **preparation is everything.**

One of the most frequent damage control calls I get is the kind received from a parent *after* this critical meeting. He went to the meeting righteously angry and resentful, yet unprepared, believing that somehow justice would be done. Weeks later, the counselor publishes a report, and it shocks and stings the parent. Sometimes, the parent hadn't understood the importance or the point of the meeting, and things went south.

The mediation process is extremely important in any *recommending* county, like San Diego. Yet, I am convinced it is the most misunderstood and underappreciated function of family court. If you have children, mediation is usually your first meeting *before* you meet a judge. During this meeting, you dialogue with a social worker. The goal is establishment of a child custody arrangement.

In "recommending counties", including San Diego, if parents can't reach an agreement in mediation, the counselor makes recommendations to the judge in your case. ***Participation in Family Court Services or private mediation is your first chance (and in most cases your best chance) to present your case to an impartial third party*** who will offer the judge input about your specifics of child custody and visitation. Often, judges adopt counselors' recommendations, with or without changes. In other words, ***what a mediation counselor recommends is likely to be a significant part of the court-ordered terms of your final divorce judgment.***

A mediation counselor's recommendations have influence, even though a judge has the final say. You only get one shot at this. There are no do-overs for mediation if you don't like the result. Being ready, really ready, for mediation is vital.

I learned early in my practice that being well prepared for mediation saved my clients stress. I have a short list of professional consultants to whom I refer clients. These caring professionals do nothing but prepare parents for mediation. Many, if not most, of these experts are themselves veterans of Family Court Services. They know what mediation counselors are looking for. These consultants, or coaches, can educate you, play devil's advocate with you and conduct a test run of the verbal sparring you're likely to experience in mediation.

Make no mistake: mediation may be quiet and seem subtle, but it nevertheless is an intellectual and emotional struggle. To forego training for it is naive. You have probably never participated in mediation before and may never do so again, but if you'll spend a little effort and money on a prep session, it will be *sooooo* worth it.

The most heartbreaking cases are those where a parent comes to me *after mediation* and hires me to do what amounts to damage control. It's tough to recover from a bad outcome in mediation. Happily, the worst results are usually preventable with knowledgeable preparation.

Preparation is the key to getting the best possible results in mediation!

> *"Give me six hours to chop down a tree and I will spend the first four sharpening the axe."*
> *Attributed to* **Abraham Lincoln by www. quotation reference.com (and by many other sources)**

We prepare ourselves for all kinds of natural disasters—earthquakes, wildfires, even tsunamis. In Southern California most of us have an escape route planned in case of a wildfire. Here in San Diego, we have marked routes along the coast in the event of a tsunami. We train to compete in sports. We realize the value of preparation in virtually every area of our lives. Yet, because we are either distracted or overwhelmed, we don't prepare for the emotional roller coaster of family court proceedings. **Don't be lulled into the naive sense that truth will prevail in your divorce or that its results will surely be fair and sensible.**

What Happens During Mediation?

Mediation usually takes place in a courthouse, but not in a courtroom. The parents and the mediation counselor meet for a couple of hours. *No lawyers, children, or witnesses are allowed to attend unless by special request of the mediation counselor.* The mediation counselor is a mental health professional who is knowledgeable about custody and visitation issues.

Each parent may be allowed to show evidence to the mediation counselor. Each county has its own local court rules about this subject. These rules are *changeable*, so be sure to *check the most recent revisions of local court rules*. Each parent explains to the mediation counselor what he or she believes to be the best parenting plan, and why.

The mediation counselor may offer you an impartial opinion about your position, then give the other parent an opinion about his or hers. Or the mediation counselor may remain poker-faced about her recommendations and tell each of you to wait for her report.

The purpose of mediation is to pull two polarized parties closer to agreement on child custody. If successful, the process helps the parents avoid the stress and expense of court. It also gives the children closure and insulates them the added emotional trauma that may otherwise befall them. When mediation is over, a shared-custody agreement is reached, not reached, or partially reached. If complete agreement isn't reached, the mediation counselor writes a report with recommendations, provides a copy of it to each parent and attorney, and files it with the court. The recommendations will include a proposed schedule, often broken down into school year versus summer break, and allocating the division of major holidays. A judge then has the final word.

What do I need to know to get the most out of the mediation session?

You should approach your mediation with the same importance that you would give to a court proceeding. **Respect your mediation counselor** *as you would a judge.* Talk about *the* children, or even better *our* children, not *my* children, and calmly describe the schedule you think works best. Be prepared to explain why. Even though you might be terribly hurt or angry, keep your emotions in check.

It can be hard to decide what to keep quiet about and what to mention during mediation. You might be aware of scandalous behavior by the other parent. You might also be shocked to find that scandalous behavior frequently does not translate to a mediation counselor as a predictor of bad parenting, and that your accusations can come across as petty at best, vindictive at worst. Gossip about adultery and kinky sexual idiosyncrasies is often considered just that. My favorite "gotcha" question from a mediation counselor: "Can you tell me something good about your spouse?" If you can't find *any* virtue in your ex-to-be, your mediation counselor is likely to conclude you're irrationally biased.

You are there to discuss the children and what's best for them, nothing else. Don't bring up finances. Parents who talk about money in mediation find it's a sure way to turn off the mediation counselor and give the impression they're more concerned about money than their children's well-being.

Your mediation counselor has influence on the outcome of your case. Don't give him the wrong impression about yourself. Mediation *can* be a stressful event, but it does not *have to* be. No matter what you do, stay calm in mediation. Wait your turn to speak and be polite. It will serve you well.

From Mediation to Orders to Judgment: Recommendations to the Court

If parents cannot reach agreement by the conclusion of mediation, and the divorce proceedings are taking place in a *recommending* county, the mediation counselor will exercise special power. In a recommending county, such as San Diego, a family court mediation counselor will make recommendations to a family court judge based on the information provided by the parents and sometimes by *collateral contacts*—teachers, doctors, therapists, et al. Copies of these recommendations will be forwarded to the parents and their attorneys. If either parent lacks a factual or legal basis for objecting to the mediation counselor's recommendations, the family court judge adopts, often verbatim, the mediation counselor's recommendations as an order of the court. **In other words, the mediation counselor's recommendations, or a modified version of them, can become terms of your temporary child custody and visitation orders and often those of your final divorce judgment.**

Preparation is so important, it's worth repeating: since the stakes are so high, professional preparation is critical. Prepare to spend a little money on your mediation. Recommendations that result from mediation will in many cases powerfully influence your final outcome.

9

DIVORCE TRIALS MEAN THINGS DIDN'T FINISH EASILY

Agree, for the law is costly.
Abraham Lincoln

Contested divorce trials occur in cases that cannot be resolved by negotiation, mediation, or collaboration. In divorce trials the disputed issues usually are child custody and visitation, property division, and child and spousal support.

When I refer to litigation in family court, I refer to any contested proceeding. It could be a pretrial motion, the trial itself or a motion that happens after the judgment has been entered. I've already discussed some pretrial motions. In the remainder of this chapter I'll be discussing trial litigation. The terms "trial" and "litigation" aren't the same thing. While trial always includes litigation, litigation doesn't always necessarily include trial.

It is now time to discuss the stage I had hoped you wouldn't have to reach. Many family law attorneys work very hard to ensure their clients don't have to go to trial.

Trial means that after much negotiation, you just haven't been able to settle on certain issues. Despite hours of work, you just haven't found a happy medium. If you must proceed to trial, each of you will leave your fate in the hands of a family court judge. You and your lawyer have likely abandoned hope of a negotiated resolution at this point.

Trial is inevitable in a case where the parties have reached an impasse on an important issue. Usually, people don't go to trial over *unimportant* issues because trial is costly, time-consuming and tedious. If you must go to trial, there is no substitute for being well prepared. When deciding *whether* to go to trial, remember that though the issues are arguable, there doesn't have to be an argu-*ment*! Reasonable minds can differ and *still* reach resolution without resorting to courtroom combat.

That's not to say that trial always or exclusively results from parties' stubbornness. A case may have unique legal or factual difficulties which cry out for new law to be made on appeal. Another case may involve issues on which expert witnesses offer contradictory opinions. I don't want to oversimplify the question of which cases go to trial.

Trial is not usually the most desirable route for divorcing parties to travel. People occasionally crave the opportunity to smear the opposition in open court, or grind the opposition into economic powder by forcing up the *opponent's* attorney's fees. When one party has engaged in unreasonable behavior resulting in reaching the impasse and therefore trial, or she offers up many baseless, or at least spurious, motions in court, her opponent will incur fees in opposing those motions. The matter can easily devolve into a war of attrition, especially when the belligerent party has a bigger war chest.

There are also the spouses who are so hurt or angry that they perversely prolong the process, and therefore the relationship, by choosing trial. Opponents in family court often have a profound sense of loss associated with the end of the case because to him or her it represents the end of the relationship. The end of a relationship in divorce is not a logical, rational event. Dragging a case out can therefore be a spouse's irrational way of avoiding – or at least delaying - a crushing sense of loss. To observers, this behavior isn't logical or objective. But it's hard to be objective when a contest is so intensely personal. This is one place where responsible lawyering comes into play—advising a client on how to manage the risks, weigh the benefits, and optimize the outcome.

One of my earliest trials involved a case where a mother refused to accept the results of two consecutive DNA tests proving that my client was not the father of her child. Predictably, the trial was brief. We subpoenaed the head of the DNA lab, whose testimony, in conjunction with other evidence, was found overwhelmingly in my client's favor. The trial was completely avoidable, but this mother insisted on having her day in court. [A subpoena is a document issued by the attorney which, if it is personally served in compliance with court rules, means the witness – the person being subpoenaed – has no choice but to show up and testify. It's a common way to safeguard against 'no-shows' at court by even the most co-operative witnesses.]

Compared to negotiating a marital settlement agreement or participating in some form of alternative resolution, trials are usually more difficult and more expensive. You'll have to pay attorney's fees for the additional time involved in preparation and presentation, along with court fees (reporter's fees at several hundred dollars per day), expert witnesses' fees, and a variety of other fees. Divorce trials also take their toll in other ways. Clients feel the emotional weight of uncertainty about the outcome and of the costs of trial, especially if they're paying by the hour. Clients need to maintain a healthy respect for the risks trial involves. The operative word is ***healthy***. Sadly, some clients become so fearful of the uncertainty of trial that they let go valuable claims in favor of getting a guaranteed result, even if it's a result not nearly as good as what they might have gotten at trial. The fear, uncertainty and costs make the decision of whether to go to trial a double-edged sword. Children are very perceptive about the toll litigation takes on their parents. Children are affected, too. Even when parents work to isolate their children from the process, children sense the anxiety produced by it. As you can see, then, divorce trials consume effort and resources, both financial and emotional.

The trial process can be long, stressful, and clumsy, even when court time is only a day or two. Getting answers on direct and cross-examination has to be one of the most inefficient means ever devised for revealing a story. But it is a time-honored tradition that has developed over hundreds of years. Witnesses testify, objections are made, sustained, and overruled. It can feel like the process is moving slowly—because it *is* moving slowly.

What can I expect to happen when I get to court?

In most divorce cases, much information is long-known to both parties—revealed well before trial through discovery or depositions. "Discovery" is a word used generically to describe several methods of finding out facts and getting documents important to the case. Among those methods are interrogatories, requests for production of documents, subpoenas, depositions and requests for admission. This short booklet will not attempt to go into greater detail about discovery. It would require a book of its own! A skilled attorney will be familiar with your trial judge's view of the law, and will know the likely result of the trial or at least be able to predict a range of likely results. But where the result depends exclusively or primarily on the *credibility* of witnesses, it's just not possible to know how a judge will rule.

Knowing the judge: How important is it? One factor that helps make the outcome in family court more predictable is when the case is assigned to one judge, permanently. The better your attorney knows the judge, the better chance you have of predicting an outcome. This is not to suggest that "knowing the judge" is equal to "influencing the judge." I mean only that a lawyer more familiar with the judge can make a better-educated guess about the outcome.

Different judges have different styles of hearing evidence, and even different views on how evidence should be interpreted. Long story short, you need to know what's most important to the judge in your case. The best family law attorneys have spent many hours observing judges' demeanor in the courtroom and noting judges' likes and dislikes. You as a layperson can no more be expected to possess this critical knowledge than for me to know what is your children's favorite food.

Work with your lawyer.

Even as you prepare for trial, your lawyer's encouragement toward settlement should be taken seriously. What a judge can award at trial is limited to what is specifically required by law or, where there is "wiggle room", what is *allowed* by law. Settlement nearly always offers more flexible options than does a trial.

Divorce trial may be necessary when an issue is truly arguable and important to one of the parties or when there are complex legal questions. By complex, I mean questions about which different appellate districts within the state have reached different conclusions, and the state Supreme Court has not yet decided; or maybe even a case of first impression – a legal question that no one has ever taken up on appeal. If you need the court of appeals to weigh in, you pretty much have to go to trial so that you have an " appealable issue." In other words, sometimes trial is unavoidable. You should do all of the following:

- **Be completely honest with your divorce attorney.** Do your best to inform your lawyer of facts that might be discovered by the other side. To be safe, don't try to guess what the other side will or won't find out on their own. Don't let your attorney be surprised in court by facts you didn't disclose. Your secrecy could cost you the case, or an important part of it.

- **Work with your attorney to designate witnesses who will provide credible testimony that supports your side of the story.** During trial, you will hopefully have witnesses who will help you explain your story. Not all witnesses are credible. Work with your attorney to get the best ones. Likewise, your witnesses have to have personal knowledge of what they're going to testify about. Don't spend much time lining up so-called "character witnesses." There usually isn't much call for character witnesses in family court. They're important mostly in criminal proceedings where a defendant risks being sentenced to prison. Each witness should be carefully chosen for the part of your story he or she is going to tell. You need to know in advance exactly what your witnesses are going to say, and your attorney needs to know who your witnesses are so he or she can talk to them long before getting to court.

- **Get documents into evidence.** This is undoubtedly the most tedious part of the process. Your attorney will have to lay a foundation for each document. This means showing the judge that a document is relevant, reliable, and otherwise admissible. Other questions have to be considered, too: What objections might be made to each document? How might the objections be overcome?

What does each document *prove*? Is there more than one way to interpret each document?

- **Forget the hope of a smoking gun or a tearful witness-stand confession.** Chances of a made-for-TV moment happening in a family court proceeding are pretty close to zero. Why? Because if the attorneys, working with their respective clients, have done their pretrial discovery (interrogatories, requests for production of documents, depositions, requests for admissions) thoroughly, there won't be any surprises sprung by either side at trial.

10

PROPERTY DIVISION:
YOUR STUFF, MY STUFF, AND OUR STUFF

Now it's time to discuss property. Property division can be difficult. One of the most common mistakes people make is thinking that *all property is community property*.

Such thinking is understandable because all property is *presumed to be community property.* "Presumptions" are common in the law, and confusing! Maybe my next book will discuss the different kinds of presumptions, but we've no room here for that conversation. For now, let's focus on this one: the presumption that applies to property being community property is a *rebuttable* presumption, one of the easiest to overcome. So ALL property is community property...until / unless it's not.

Not all property is community property, and knowing what is and isn't will save you emotional stress as well as dollars and cents.

You'll need to make up your mind about what is worth going to the mat over, and what isn't going to be that important six months, a year, or five years from now. I once had a client tell me he had a sentimental attachment to the Coleman camping cooler. Strangely, his wife also shared that attachment. He wouldn't sign a marital settlement agreement that did not award him the gear. Each spouse incurred hundreds of dollars in attorney's fees – with each lawyer urging his client to throw in the towel already! - arguing over an asset worth less than a hundred dollars. He ultimately let her keep the gear. As a rule of thumb, if you can replace it easily, let it go.

One of the most basic issues you will face during your divorce is that of property and debt. This involves dividing and assigning: dividing *marital*—community—property between two recipients, and assigning *separate* property to the rightful, single recipient.

All property falls into one of three categories: (1) community property, (2) separate property, and (3) mixed property.

One of your earliest homework assignments will be listing for your family law attorney all property involved and gathering information and documentation to help figure out what it's worth. Then you'll suggest how **you** would like to split it up. Sometimes spouses get lucky and their wish lists completely or mostly coincide. That your lists coincide even somewhat is better than them not coinciding at all.

If your wish lists intersect very little or not at all, not to worry overmuch: there are ways to figure it out. Sometimes the biggest disagreements are about **worth**. Other times, they're about **who gets what**. Sometimes an asset isn't worth discussing at all. Thinking about the value of each asset keeps in perspective the importance of whether you end up with it.

Marital property division.

Community property: each gets half, right? What could be simpler? Ah, if only it were that simple. California is a *community property* state. Different states use different approaches to division of marital property, but in a community property state like California, *if spouses cannot agree* on property division, a family court judge will award each *one half* of the community property interests acquired. Community property is different from *separate property*, and we'll spend some time talking about each.

The most common forms of separate property are:
- Property a spouse owned before marriage.
- Gifts a spouse received at any time.
- Inheritance a spouse received at **any** time.
- Property that the spouses agree in writing is separate, as long as the wording meets California's standards.
- Property acquired (1) by one spouse (2) using another separate property asset (3) with the intention of keeping it separate. (Example: a spouse spends part of his inheritance to buy a car, the title to which is in his name only.)
- Certain personal injury awards. (In general, the portion of the award that compensates for lost earnings is marital property, while any portion for pain and suffering is separate property.)

Mixed property is partly community and partly separate.

The differences between these kinds of property – community, separate and mixed - define collectively the *character* or *characterization* of the property. The character of property can be hotly debated. The most common mixed properties are real estate and pension or retirement plans. It gets complicated! If a home owned by one spouse before marriage is refinanced during marriage, and a feature of the refinancing is the addition of the other spouse to the home's title, is the home separate or community property? Um…Yes? Actually, it's likely *both*. A typical pension example would be one where a spouse worked as a teacher several years before marrying, worked fifteen years while married, and expects to work another ten years after divorce. Here again is an asset—pension—that is partly the teacher's separate property and partly community property.

Working it all out: who gets what?

Most people are able to agree on some, if not most, property issues without going to court. When people do go to court for property division, it's because they can't agree on who gets property or what it is worth.

Some people are able to agree, easily, by sitting at the kitchen table. They make detailed lists; they have up-to-date files. These ultra-organized couples are enviable. They not only can agree on the facts but also can have a civilized conversation, even while the world as they know it comes to an end. They are in a minority. Most people's cases require a bit more effort and help to work things out. Because there is more to the property division process than just doing the math on a spreadsheet, I recommend professional help. The majority of spouses assume *all property* is community property. That assumption can result in huge errors and missed opportunities to rightfully claim assets as *separate property*. It's not the arithmetic that trips people up most; it's not knowing in which column the numbers belong.

Understanding the law is important. California community property law was designed to make things simpler by creating a presumption that all property is community property. But there are so many exceptions (i.e. to the presumption that all property is community property) that make property matters complex. For example, some assets will be presumed to be whatever "character" (community, separate or other) the title to the asset says, regardless of when it was acquired or with what. *Community property* is generally property acquired during the marriage with money earned during the marriage, and it gets split fifty-fifty. A few of the factors that foul up that very simple formula are gifts; inheritances or transfers of real estate during marriage; and assets acquired partly before and partly during marriage, or partly during and partly after separation.

Even though it can be a real hassle to list everything you own, put a value on it, and come up with a plan for dividing it, it's a necessary part of the process. One of the benefits of avoiding court is that it's okay if you agree on dividing property or debts in a way that's not exactly equal. Outside court, there's no rule that says you have to do things the way a judge would.

Marital Property Division: the Basics

Property division is complicated, even for experts. You shouldn't assume that because division worked out one way in Uncle Joe's case (which you know all about), it will work out similarly in a different scenario—e.g., your own. We all know that if we run a stop sign in front of a police officer, we're going to get cited. The tendency is to think *all* law works sensibly and simply this way—which couldn't be more mistaken. In property division, the devil is most certainly in the details.

Educating yourself on the different kinds of property interests will help you feel more in control when negotiating toward settlement. Here are the basic principles involved in a few of the most common property division issues in California.

- **REAL ESTATE:** Sometimes, even now, there actually is equity in real estate. The simplest situation is where the property in question was bought during the marriage with down payment money earned during the marriage, and whose mortgage payments were made with money earned during the marriage. That's easy. Either the property is sold and the proceeds are split evenly, or one spouse buys out the other. Practically speaking, buyouts are hard these days because they require the buying spouse to refinance. Establishing a healthy loan-to-value ratio for lenders is now harder than ever. Still, at least in theory, this situation where the property is without a doubt community property and gets resolved by sale or buy-out is the simplest scenario.

- The second-simplest situation is where one of you owned the property in question before you got hitched, and the title has remained in the original owner's name. Some fancy math is needed to figure out whether the non-owner spouse should get some of the equity, but once all the necessary raw numbers are known, a good attorney can provide an accurate calculation. If real estate was once owned by one spouse but now has a title that lists both, or if it was once owned by both spouses but now has a title that lists only one, property division is much more complicated. Don't assume there is a black-and-white answer to the real estate title scenario above involving *mixed property.*

- **HOUSEHOLD STUFF:** You've got a new life to start living. Don't let this stuff get in your way. Household items aren't usually worth arguing about. I have seen at least one divorce where the husband and wife argued for an hour, attorneys present, about who got the thirty-five-dollar camping cooler (see above). Don't get distracted by low-value stuff. Many household items can be replaced quickly and cheaply at garage sales and through Craigslist, eBay, and other places.

- **VEHICLES:** Cars, trucks, motorcycles, boats, etc. All must be valued according to Kelley Blue Book, NADA, or another third-party source. Most of the time, but not always, there is no equity in vehicles involved because more is owed on them than they are worth. California family lawyers know that local court rules set the standards for figuring out the value of vehicles. There is at

63

least one simple part of this, however: whoever gets awarded a vehicle gets responsibility for the vehicle's loan.

- **RETIREMENT PLANS:** Dividing 401(k) plans, private pensions, and public or government retirement plans can be challenging. Or not.

Most pension plans can be divided using a formula that works like this: whatever was accumulated during marriage is community; whatever was accumulated before marriage and after separation is separate, belonging to the spouse who earned it.

Often the retirement account–s date-of-marriage balance can be subtracted from its date-of-separation balance and–voilà!–you have the community interest.

Value of 401(k) on date of separation minus value of 401(k) on date of marriage equals community value of 401(k).

Let's say a wife works at Qualcomm and had $100,000 in her 401(k) before marrying. After continued contributions, her 401(k) contains $300,000 at the time she separates from her husband. Community property totals $200,000.

Things get complicated when a retirement account contains financial products of fluctuating value, such as stock and stock options. Actuaries and accountants are then better suited for the calculation. For example, say our wife in the above scenario had a Qualcomm retirement portfolio valued at $300,000 on the date of separation, but (1) she made postseparation contributions to it, and (2) the market went up (or down!) dramatically after the date of separation. The questions are tougher here. For example, if the community interest on the date of separation is known to be $300,000, the wife subsequently contributed postseparation earnings (separation property), and the account at the time of divorce is worth $500,000 instead of $300,000, how much of it is community property?

In the case of a retirement that depends on length of service, the "time rule" would apply. Common examples are military and teachers' retirement. **Here's how the time rule works:**

Divorces involving one or two military service members are fairly common in San Diego due to the number of sailors and Marines here. The rules can be understood while keeping the math simple.

*Assume a service-member spouse was single before enlisting in the Navy, served for five years, got married, separated from her spouse after ten years of marriage, and retired from the Navy at twenty years of service. That makes five years of service **before marriage** and five years of service **after separation**.*

In this scenario our sailor has ten years' worth of separate-property retirement—for the five years before marriage and the five years after separation. There is ten years' worth of community property, too—for the sailor's ten years of service during marriage.

Ten years, or 120 months, of service during marriage means half the interest is community. There are twenty years, or 240 months, of service in total. Each spouse receives half of the amount built up during marriage, and the service member gets everything else. In this scenario, the service-member gets ¾ of the retirement pay: *all* of the separate property portion, and half of the community property portion.

11

WHO GETS THE DEBTS?

What is important to you? What amount can you live on? Be prepared to live on less, because after divorce there are two households instead of one. Often, there isn't enough money to go around *before* separation. The period before divorce is a good time to document your debt and expenses. Most people lose track of what has been paid for and what things cost. This is your chance to think about your future income and what amount you will need to live on. The division of debt affects the final property division decision made in your divorce case.

There are two types of debt, not including tax debt, which belongs in a class by itself: *secured debt* (like a mortgage secured by your home or a loan secured by your vehicle) and *unsecured debt* (like credit card balances, unpaid medical bills, and other personal obligations).

Am I Responsible for My Spouse's Debts After Divorce?

Maybe! Just like property, debts fall into three categories: *(1) community, (2) separate, and (3) mixed*, which is partly community and partly separate.

Community debt. Let's say you and your spouse bought a house during marriage, and the down payment came from savings accumulated during marriage. At last, a no-brainer. This debt is 100 percent community debt.

Separate debt: Let's say your spouse owed a boatload of debt prior to marriage and has been unable to pay it off. Assume you haven't signed as a cosigner or guarantor on any of the debt. Does your marriage to the debtor make this debt community debt? Happily, the answer is no. Debt acquired by a spouse prior to marriage, just like property similarly acquired, remains the separate property of the spouse.

Your divorce: not really a get-out-of-jail-free card.

- Your divorce won't get rid of your legal duty to pay community debts. Even if your divorce judgment gives your spouse responsibility to pay a certain debt, it won't relieve you of your obligation for a debt that you've signed on as either the account holder or as a cosigner. If a lender has a contract that contains your signature and says you agree to pay a debt, the lender can ignore any deal you and your spouse make regarding who has to pay the debt. Let's say you make a deal that provides your spouse has to pay the Capital One card. If your spouse fails to keep up debt payments, Capital One can still come after you. Some really ambitious creditors may enforce against you an obligation to pay for debts for "necessities of life" incurred by the other spouse. The law is on the side of the creditor in that case.

- A judgment of divorce is a deal between former spouses, *not* between former spouses and their creditors. Even if you and your spouse agree about how property and debt should be divided, creditors may have different ideas.

- **Student loans** are usually assigned to student spouses except in *some* cases, where loans were taken out more than ten years before the date of separation. The idea is that if the couple stuck together that long after the debt was incurred, the community presumably got its money's worth out of the education financed by the loan.

- **Even if you don't know about them, debts incurred during marriage are still community debts.** The rudest awakenings are experienced by the unsuspecting spouses of secretive compulsive gamblers and shopaholics. It doesn't seem fair, I know. But those gambling debts are community debts. Sometimes one spouse is a more enthusiastic spender than the other. When a Schedule of Assets and Debts arrives showing credit card debt concealed for months or years by the spending spouse, the effect is a sinking feeling coupled with anger and resentment.

Bankruptcy First, Then Divorce?
If you're deep in debt and need a divorce, timing can be everything. In some instances, spouses can gain an advantage by filing bankruptcy jointly rather than separately. In other instances it's just the opposite—one spouse may need an obligation to pay court-ordered support to the other spouse to qualify for bankruptcy. A competent

bankruptcy attorney can tell you which approach will work best.

Remember that no one gets out of paying child support by filing bankruptcy.

In fact, spousal support and child support are *priority debts* and must be given priority over other debts in a Chapter 13 bankruptcy plan. Support arrears are not dischargeable in bankruptcy. In some instances, bankruptcy can reduce **payments** on *arrears* (but not on the ongoing fixed monthly amount), but support **debt itself** will never be wiped away.

How does bankruptcy court figure out which part of your obligation to your spouse is for support and which part is for property settlement? Different courts use different criteria to answer this question, but the important thing to remember is this: *if the obligation in question is for support, it's not dischargeable.* In Chapter 13 some property settlement obligations *can* be discharged. If you are considering an attempt – or need to oppose an attempt by the other spouse - to get rid of a duty to pay money called for in a divorce judgment, tread carefully and get representation from a knowledgeable bankruptcy attorney.

For this reason give careful consideration to any agreements that divide debt between you and your spouse. Your family law attorney can help you look at all the factors in your case, including your post-divorce financial resources, and devise a plan for assigning debts. If financial counseling is needed, or if you must consider bankruptcy, your attorney will likely know where to refer you.

12

SPOUSAL SUPPORT:
ARE THERE ANY RULES?

Spousal support has spawned a variety of urban legends—you know, stories that are widely believed but not really true. Before you decide whether to make an issue of spousal support, you need to be fully up to date about the subject.

What is spousal support?

Spousal support is money paid by one spouse to the other to make up for a difference in income. The goal, at least initially, when *temporary spousal support* is awarded, is to keep both spouses at a standard of living similar to the one they enjoyed before divorce. Different objectives are addressed when *permanent spousal support* orders are made.

Spousal support is not awarded in every divorce, but its use is not obsolete. A common mistake people make when not represented by an attorney is giving up too much or too soon on spousal support. Too many people are unintentionally generous when giving up spousal support rights for the sake of getting things over with and moving on. The inverse is also true, though: some unreasonably hold out for a spousal support order that is highly unlikely to ever materialize.

Here is a real-life example: A husband is earning about $100,000 a year, and he wants avoid paying alimony. Neither spouse is represented by an attorney. The husband's estranged wife, a clerical worker, earns about $20,000 / year. She verbally agrees to $400 a month in alimony, after a twenty-year marriage. This case is an example of a huge discrepancy between what a spouse *is* receiving and what she *could be* receiving. In this case, the wife doesn't want to make waves. She is leaving on the table as much as $2000 a month because she simply doesn't want to rock the boat and make things more difficult. It's okay to leave money on the table. At least *know* that you're doing so. When I'm representing the supported spouse, I like to include language in the agreement or judgment that explains clearly what the client is giving up, and why. Only a competent lawyer can give you straight talk on the issue of spousal support. Guesswork is too risky.

How Long Will Spousal Support Be Paid?

If a judge decides it's appropriate to award spousal support, it will be awarded for a **reasonable period** of time, *with a view toward getting the recipient to a point where he is self-supporting.* A very flexible rule, only applied in marriages of less than ten years, provides that spousal support shouldn't go on for longer than half the length of the marriage. [This rule is found in California Family Code Section 4320.] Don't count on it as an absolute. A court can order spousal support for a longer or shorter time, depending on what the facts of the case call for. Spousal support is a hugely negotiable point in family law.

So how do you know if you risk having to pay, or are entitled to receive, spousal support? Assuming you and your spouse can't agree about it, a family court judge will look at several things. My favorites are listed below. The rest can be found in California Family Code Section 4320.

- The extent to which you and your spouse have enough earning capacity to maintain the *standard of living established during marriage*.
- Whether the spouse asking for support helped the higher-paid spouse get a better job by *contributing to his education, training, or professional license.* **"Contributing" is broadly interpreted, but often means taking primary responsibility for the children while the other spouse focuses on career / education.**
- Whether the spouse being asked for support has the *ability to pay* without experiencing a change in the marital standard of living.
- What each spouse *needs* in order to keep up the marital standard of living.
- The *assets and debts* of each spouse after divorce.
- The *length of marriage.*
- The support-seeking spouse's *ability to work* and whether work would interfere with child-rearing responsibilities.
- Any *domestic violence* committed by one spouse against the other.

- The **tax consequences** and **economic hardships** that spousal support would have and cause.
- Whether childless parties can get by just fine on what they have.

How Much Spousal Support Will Be Ordered?

There are two kinds of spousal support: **temporary spousal support** and **permanent spousal support**. Temporary spousal support, ordered while a divorce is underway, lasts until permanent spousal support is ordered at trial or in a final judgment. Permanent spousal support usually lasts longest; it is paid indefinitely or for a specified period of time after divorce. For each kind of support, differing rules apply when figuring out how much, and for how long, support will be paid.

Calculating exactly how much support will be paid is tricky. The result of calculation is only as good as the data available and the skill of the person performing the calculation. Ultimately, it can come down to a judge's subjective opinion (*discretion*) about what's right and just.

The awarding of spousal support can be left up to a judge, but is also negotiable. Here are some guidelines.

- Generally, the greater the difference in income, the more likely that spousal support will be ordered, and the higher the support amount will be.
- Sometimes a judge will order permanent spousal support to be paid for a period equal to about half the length of the marriage.
- Other times the judge may order permanent spousal support to be paid when there is not a

great difference in income, or for a period longer than half the length of the marriage, in cases where minor children will be living with the support-seeking spouse. The awarding of support is nearly completely within a judge's discretion, and is dependent on the specific facts of the case.

Spousal support is highly dependent on a the impression made on a judge, The best result happens when the judge can find lots of reasons to like you and approve of the way you've handled yourself in the litigation. Conversely, those who give the judge reasons to be displeased with them may find themselves being disfavored on discretionary issues (like spousal support).

13

CHILD CUSTODY AND VISITATION

Entire books have been written about child custody and visitation. This won't be one of them, but it will introduce you to some basics and, hopefully, help prevent some common awkward moments in family court.

We're going to talk about three common misunderstandings concerning custody. Here they are, exemplified by what clients say they want.

- **I want full custody. (What the clients mean is that they want *sole* custody, since "full" custody doesn't actually exist.)**

At one time, sole legal custody was a fairly common arrangement. However, for many years courts nationwide have been steering away from sole legal custody arrangements. These days, a California family court judge is unlikely to order sole legal custody.

When do courts award sole legal custody?

Family courts order sole legal custody when it is clear that joint legal custody would be dangerous or unworkable. Joint legal custody is not in the best interests of the children when one parent has a history of abuse, neglect, domestic violence, or other dangerous behavior. The risk of harm to the children has to be real, not just speculative or feared, in order to persuade a judge that sole custody is the answer (or at least part of the answer) to the dispute. If a judge finds the parents are unlikely to agree on *anything*, she may order a parent's sole legal custody just to avoid an impasse and ensure decisions are made. Unfortunately, well-meaning parents can disagree so vehemently that they behave like politicians in an election year, polarized for the sake of polarization. Thankfully, these cases are rare.

Joint legal custody: the most common solution.

Your divorce is probably going to result in an order for ***joint legal custody***. It's the most commonly ordered kind of legal custody in California. In this arrangement, each parent ***participates equally in the decision making*** regarding the children's ***health, education, and welfare***.

- **When it comes to physical custody, I want fifty-fifty.**

Whenever I hear *anyone* say this, I wince. It's not that fifty-fifty is a bad thing; it's just that a parent will gravitate to it because it seems fair to her. Therein lies the problem; the parent is focused on what is fair to *her*. No parent wants to lose precious time with her children, or feel like she has to be a winner and the other parent a loser. In the end, the parenting plan may be somewhat lopsided and adaptable, depending on the best interests of the children.

When our son was young, I was a stay-at-home parent (and law student) and thus spent more time with him than did my wife. As the years passed and our lives changed, my wife's work schedule changed and I went to work. Our roles reversed. Had we separated then, you can see why an adjustment of the parenting plan would have been best for our child.

Joint <u>physical</u> custody is also more common than sole physical custody. Joint physical custody is commonly misunderstood to mean equal custody. It doesn't. It *does* mean children spend a significant amount of time with each parent. It isn't uncommon for an order to **say** the parents have joint physical custody, but go on to describe a parenting plan which places the children with one parent the majority of the time. The court's priority—its only priority—is what's best for the children.

The parenting plan sets out the children's schedule—how their time is divided between the parents. Pretty much any arrangement other than sole physical custody can be characterized as joint physical custody.

What factors are considered in choosing a custody arrangement?

A family court (i.e., a judge) will order a custody arrangement that *it* believes is in **the best interests of the children,** a broad legal standard used in one form or another in almost every state. When deciding your child custody case, a court has latitude to order what it believes is in the children's best interests based on the **unique facts of your case**. A judge will look at several factors that can affect her child custody decision. **The most important are**:

- **The status quo.** *Stability and continuity for the children is a big priority*; the court's goal is to minimize the level of disruption the children experience as a result of the divorce. For this reason a court will look at established patterns, like where and with whom the children have been living. Your judge will be hesitant to disrupt the children's lives by ordering a change in those patterns unless there's good reason to do so. The flip side of this principle is that in some cases the *status quo* is so bad for the children that the *status quo* is *itself* the most powerful argument for changing it.

- **Parenting skills.** Generally, a court will assume that each parent is competent. If you really feel it is appropriate to challenge an assessment of your spouse's ability to care for the children or make decisions about them, you can and, in the right circumstances, should. A family law attorney can give you the best advice about whether the facts of your case justify efforts to discredit your spouse's parenting credentials.

- **Other factors.** The ages of the children; the strength of their bonds with each parent; how they are faring under the pre–custody order arrangement; conflicts among them, input from a treating therapist or *special master* or *custody* *evaluator* (a therapist or psychologist); and other facts that help a judge figure out what kind of schedule is going will work best for the children will be taken into consideration.

"My situation is just like my cousin Dave's when he got divorced. So the outcome should be the same, right?" Probably not.

A man we'll call Joe once sat down with me for a conversation about his situation, and explained that his was, indeed, just like "Dave's." "How so,?" I asked? "Well, we've both been married twelve years and we both have two children, ages six and eight. Dave has fifty-fifty custody with his ex. *And* Dave is getting child support. So that's what I should get."

The more we talked, the more apparent it became that the differences between their two situations were far more instructive than were the similarities. Dave lived five doors down from his ex, so the children don't didn't even have to cross the street to get from one parent's house to the other. Dave's ex was a surgeon earning $500,000 / a year, while Dave holds held down a middle middle-management position earning about $80,000. And Joe's wife has had been a stay-at-home mother for the past five years, while Joe (like his friend Dave) worked in a sister department of the same company that employed Dave. Joe's salary: $80,000 / a year.

You get the picture. Matters of Family Court and family law are rarely as cut and dried as many other matters of other law. Take breach of contract, for example. Somebody who owes money doesn't pay. His lender sues and gets a judgment for the balance owed. End of story. Consider DUI, for example. A motorist is pulled over and found to have a blood-alcohol level of 0.09% percent. He's been driving under the influence. Likely he'll be convicted. The point I'm making is that comparing *your family law* situation with someone else's is never a good idea. Cases are almost never as simple as you'd hope.

A judge's broad power and the focus on the unique facts of your case mean that ***no two custody cases are ever alike***. The days when mothers could count on (and fathers would fear) an automatic alternating-weekend schedule are long gone. This is one of the reasons that it is so important to obtain legal advice about child custody. Avoid consulting sources like generic legal information websites and barber shop or water cooler lawyers (laypeople) who offer inaccurate "legal" opinions about what to do in your case). I have done a considerable amount of damage control for parents who have made legal claims based on "water cooler" legal advice. Consider the stakes : your relationship with your children. As any attorney can tell you it is always easier to prevent a legal problem than to clean up the mess which develops if one isn't nipped in the bud. An ounce of prevention…

How Does Visitation Work?

"Frequent and continuous" contact with each parent" is the mantra of the Family Code.

In any divorce that involves children, a nearly limitless number of *visitation arrangements* is possible. Spouses who come to an amicable settlement agreement regarding custody and visitation can craft arrangements that are specific to their unique situation.

One parent may be tempted to try to limit the other's access to the children for the wrong reasons. It's fairly common, and sometimes quite justifiable, for a parent ending a marriage to be angry, hurt and resentful toward the other parent. Be aware that a judge will look for ways to ensure that the children have access to each parent that make sense. Fighting to keep the children away from the other parent is a common mistake. It escalates legal fees, and unless your cause has compelling merit, it's likely to be futile.

Visitation arrangements range from absolutely no visitation to whatever visitation is mutually agreed upon. *Court orders for zero visitation are not common.* Zero-visitation orders almost always result from a parent's history of *domestic violence, substance abuse, child abuse, serious neglect, or child molestation*.

If emotions are to run high in family court, they usually run *highest* at the beginning of a case. The result is that spouses are ready to do their worst to each other and feel entitled, even duty bound, to punish each other by limiting access to the children. The mix of parents' great sense of responsibility toward their children and their anger and resentment toward one another can make for strange and powerful rationalizations for treating Family

Court as a forum for competition. In the most contentious cases it's no holds barred.

There are, unfortunately, parents who see custody and visitation litigation as a forum in which to do battle with the enemy. When this happens, naturally the level of conflict goes sky-high. When elevated levels of conflict are involved, cases become extremely time-consuming and generate first dozens, then hundreds of billable hours. Really.

Let's talk about some of the more common visitation arrangements. It's often not feasible to arrange for school-age children to stay overnight several times per week with a noncustodial parent. A more typical arrangement is for children to spend alternating weekends, along with one or maybe two midweek overnights every week with the noncustodial parent. This arrangement may be more highly varied in cases involving younger children.

In extraordinary cases where the parents live close to one another and transportation time between homes is minimal, a true fifty-fifty parenting arrangement may easily be manageable. It should be understood, however, that such an arrangement is the exception, not the rule. Often, managing a fifty-fifty plan is too disruptive for the children, just because of the logistics. Parents who live on opposite ends of a county, for example, would have a tough time. Much of the children's time would be spent commuting.

Visitation arrangements differ from case to case as much as necessary. Parents are far better served crafting their own arrangement with creativity and cooperation than by having a judge figure out an arrangement for them.

What happens when parents live on opposite sides of the country?

Deciding on a visitation schedule in the increasingly common situation where parents live a considerable distance from each other—in different states, or perhaps across the continent—is in some ways *easier* than doing so with both parents local. Long-distance visitation is determined more by finances and logistics than perhaps anything else. A typical arrangement in such a situation is for the children to spend alternating major holidays with each parent and half to nearly all summer nonschool time with the noncustodial parent. A variant where money and logistics permit is for the children to spend one weekend per month, and sometimes all three-day weekends with the noncustodial parent.

From Agreement to Judgment

By the time you appear before a judge, you will have spent a great deal of time working on resolving issues like child custody. Step one involves the initial negotiations after your divorce is filed. Step two, taken if the initial negotiations do not result in agreement, involves mediation.

If you reach agreement as a result of step one or two, court appearance will likely be unnecessary or a smooth experience. **When parties agree in writing to a**

resolution of all issues, court appearance may not be required. Instead, an MSA (marital settlement agreement) is drafted, then reviewed (and often revised along the way) and signed by all parties. It might also be signed by their respective attorneys. Next, a judgment along with the MSA and other documents is submitted to the clerk's office and signed by the judge (really by a clerk who stamps the judge's signature) and you're done!

If you wind up having to go to court, and an agreement *has* been *reached but not yet signed*, you won't have to rehash the facts or legal arguments of your case. All you'll have to do is tell the judge you have reached an agreement and that you want your agreement to become an order of the court. While family court judges have the final say on custody orders, agreements are almost always accepted and incorporated as part of a final judgments. On financial issues like splitting up property and debt or determining spousal support, you can expect the judge to go along with your agreement.

14

CHILD SUPPORT: WHO PAYS? HOW MUCH WILL IT BE?

Child support is mandatory if a parent asks a family court judge to order it and the evidence calls for it. Results of child support hearings are among the most predictable of family court proceedings. At least the math is certain. The data goes into a formula, a number comes out, and that number is what the judge must order, with only rare exceptions.

But don't jump the gun. Presenting and arguing for data that goes—or should go—into the formula is a matter where a great number of people need help.

The consequences of error in child support calculation can be long-lasting; even a few hundred dollars per month can add up to a lot of lost money over a period of years.

I can't count the number of times I've been asked to finish a case started by someone else—usually a non-attorney—and have discovered big mistakes in how child support was handled. In many of those cases, some form of free online support calculator was used. Some calculators are better than others, but they all have two things in common: the result is only as good as the data that gets input, and their misuse by non-attorneys is the rule, not the exception.

Judges do a good job of working with the data they have. Nevertheless, I always take my laptop to court with me so I can backstop the calculation and, sometimes, to offer the court assistance. The data they have, though, may be seriously incomplete and judges thus may order the wrong amount of support, lacking the right information. I know of some parents who have even entered into agreements for set amounts, relying on inaccurate calculations one of them came up with on some free online calculator. Ordinarily, that's the result of operator error. "Penny-wise and pound-foolish" is the phrase that comes to mind. Once a child support amount is ordered, it's not always easy to get it modified. It's worth your time to consult with an attorney who can ensure that you get the amount right the first time.

What goes into the formula? Each parent's income and the amount of time the children spend with each parent. Seems simple, right?

In theory, it is. In practice, calculating child support can be anything but simple. You may know that a non-custodial parent's *child-share* time is figured out and a *percentage* assigned to it, **but do you know what legally counts as child-share time?**

Common sense in family law doesn't always work.

Using common sense isn't always helpful in family court. For instance, you might think a child's time at school shouldn't be counted toward time with a parent. After all, the child is in class, in childcare, or at camp, and no parent is hovering nearby, directly caring for the child. But you'd be wrong. Time with the parent who *doesn't* have primary physical custody of the child is added up, and the resulting sum may or may not include school time. Usually, no school time is allotted to the noncustodial parent. All time not specifically allocated to the noncustodial parent is, by default, allocated to the custodial parent. That typically means hours spent in school are allocated to the custodial parent. But don't despair if you're the noncustodial parent. It's worth making the argument that some school time should be allocated to you. The judge *can* allocate some of the time to you under certain circumstances.

Assume a noncustodial parent has alternating weekends with his child, a child-share time of about 15 percent. *All other time* (i.e., 85 percent of the total) is assigned to the *custodial parent*. Is this fair, when children spend thirty-five to forty hours per week in school? School time alone amounts to about 25 percent of a week, and about half of all waking hours. What about sleep time? That gets credited to the parent at whose home the child sleeps. Is all this fair? I won't try to answer that here. What's most important before contemplating divorce is for you to know what you're dealing with so you can make well-informed decisions.

Visitation: Do you have to "pay to play?"

Another classic example of a mistake people make in the way they think about child support is believing that payment of child support purchases visitation time. Parents may be making this mistake if they've said something like this:

> *He's not paying child support, so I'm not going to let him have the kids this weekend.*

Or there's the flip side:

> *She won't let me see the kids, so I'm not going to pay child support.*

Bottom line: The right of a parent to see his children exists even when he is behind on child support. Likewise, the duty to pay child support remains even when the support recipient is frustrating visitation.

What happens when a parent doesn't follow the rules?

If the other parent is not complying with the terms of a court order for visitation, child support, or another issue, your remedy is not to violate the court order yourself. Your remedy is to return to court and ask for enforcement of the order.

If you are court-ordered to make your children available for visitation but do not, you risk punishment for contempt of court. If you are able to pay child support and are court-ordered to do so, but do not, you also risk such punishment. Contempt can mean fines and jail time.

Really. Jail time can be up to five days for each count of which the defendant is convicted, and he's still on the hook for the support.

15

URBAN LEGENDS AND DIVORCE:
IT JUST AIN'T SO

During nearly two decades of practice in family law, I have heard the same threats, objections, and protests repeatedly. I call their underlying beliefs urban legends: false, but nevertheless touted as truth. I hope that by reading these statements, based on urban legends in family law, you can learn to tell real risks apart from imaginary ones.

1. **"I'll quit my job before I pay you that much support."** Not likely the party making this threat will actually make good on it. This is usually an attempt by one spouse to bluff the other into agreeing to a lower support amount. Ask your attorney whether you should call this bluff. Document the statement right away. Write down the date, circumstances, and exact words used. Better yet, if your spouse sends you this statement by e-mail or letter, save it for use as evidence. Judges do not tolerate this kind of bullying, and they have powerful ways of sending spouses the message.

2. **"It doesn't make sense for us to pay two lawyers; it's a waste of money that we could otherwise keep. Let's both just use mine."** Aside from the obvious conflict of interest this arrangement

would create, a spouse making this plea wants to control the other and the divorce process by influencing the quantity and quality of advice given you. Don't fall for this. Good legal advice and representation may not be inexpensive, but its value is priceless.

3. **"You have no right to take what's mine away from me."** This statement usually refers to a pension or right to a retirement account. The error in it is that a pension / retirement right is not owned by only one spouse; pension earned during the marriage belongs to both spouses. Your request for half of what was generated during the marriage is fair, and the law entitles you to it.

4. **"I'm taking the children to North Carolina/Texas/some other place and filing the case there."** If your spouse makes this threat and actually does move, she might get away with it, at least in part, unless you go to court quickly. There is one controlling law that says which state's courts can make orders regarding custody and visitation. It's called the Uniform Child Custody Jurisdiction and Enforcement Act. It is a much-misunderstood federal statute. At the first sign that you are at risk of having more than one state claiming its court can make custody and visitation orders, get professional legal advice.

5. **"You'll never see the children again."** This is usually part of an attempt to get a spouse to stay in the relationship. California law presumes that children's frequent and continuing contact with

both parents is a good thing, so this threat is seldom legitimate.

6. **"Your attorney is just running up your bill demanding all these documents of me. Call him off."** Any family law attorney will need to see documents that relate to you and your spouse's finances. Otherwise he can't say what you should expect or demand. Talk with your lawyer about what *you* want to see. Don't have your attorney issue a boilerplate demand for production of documents listing dozens of things you know don't exist, or that you already have. Some attorneys take a shotgun approach to litigation, employing a wide blast of discovery – demand for production of documents, form interrogatories, deposition, requests for admissions, etc., even when their client already knows or has much of the information and documents that would be responsive to these discovery requests. A more specific *surgical* approach is faster, less expensive and more effective. It's just awfully tempting for a lawyer to avoid thinking through what he / she actually *needs* the other side to produce. It's much easier to strike a couple of macros on one's keyboard, even when that generates needless work. Be sure and participate with your attorney in the decisions about what discovery you do, and do not feel is needed.

7. **"You didn't work a day during our marriage; you just stayed home and took care of the kids. Hell will freeze over before you get a dime of my retirement."** A spouse making this threat has no

power to make good on it, since a court can and will simply order that a retirement plan administrator pay the stay-at-home parent that portion of the retirement benefits she's due.

8. **"I'll go to jail before I pay support to you."** A warning about jail time is among several tools judges have available to enforce support orders, but such a warning is seldom necessary. A spouse's jail threat is a common bluff. It's easy for a judge to get anyone with a paycheck to pay support involuntarily, so most people just pay it.

9. **"I'll only pay support if I know the money is going to the children. I want receipts for everything you spend that child-support check on."** California law does not require supported parents to give account to supporting parents for how support money is spent—period. It's not appropriate to demand or offer such micro-management.

10. **"If the court finds out how you've behaved, you'll never see the children."** In other words, "Back off or the mudslinging begins." Family court judges aren't outraged by the same things spouses are. Histories of promiscuity, several-years-past drug habits, infidelity, and moderate drinking are things judges realize don't reflect poorly on parenting ability, so judges don't take them into account. It's fairly common for one party to allege the other has a substance *abuse* (not just *use*) problem. Addiction and dependency, though, *are* problems for any parent involved in family court proceedings.

11. **"We'll do this like I say, or else."** This threat is usually capped off with a threat of withholding support and sometimes a veiled or direct threat of physical harm. Law exists to ensure justice and fairness are exercised when adversaries are of unequal strength, funding, and sophistication. The divorce process works if you let it. Let it work for you. Leveling the playing field can be slow and frustrating work, but it usually *can* be done.

12. **"I'll litigate you into bankruptcy. I'd rather pay my lawyer than yours, so don't expect me to compromise on anything."** Many spouses make this threat hoping their opponents will give up and run. While it is unfortunate that people use such tactics, techniques may be deployed to stop spouses from making good on this threat. A good attorney can push a case forward to conclusion even over the objections of a party determined to delay and complicate the process. Then, the court can sanction (fine) the unreasonable spouse who is using these tactics. The most common form of sanction is to order the unreasonable spouse to pay part – or all – of the other's attorney's fees.

16

AFTER THE END: THE LEGAL UPS AND DOWNS AFTER DIVORCE

After the dust has settled and everyone has gotten into the parenting and support routine, things can happen that stir some (or all) of it up again. Someone gets angry, another loses his job, a working ex-spouse gets transferred, and one ex-spouse starts dating and the other gets jealous. The list is endless.

Things change. What are you going to do? How are you going to respond?

Motions for modification of court orders are fairly common in family court.

Modification of what, and why, you ask? The most commonly modified orders are those concerning spousal support, child support, child custody, and child visitation. Most things are pretty much final once a judgment is filed with the court. But, for *good cause* based on a *material change of circumstances*, a party might ask a court to change certain existing orders.

The result can be a sort of minitrial that may involve testimony, including that of psychologists; financial records; and the procedural complications that go with trial, including objections and argument. Don't underestimate the importance of these motions. *Postjudgment* has an "afterthought" ring to it, but postjudgment motions are anything but mere afterthought. Just because they happen after the final judgment is entered doesn't mean they can't still be life-changing events. The majority of move-away motions, for example, in cases where one parent is moving far enough away from the other that visitation logistics will be affected, are made *after* the final judgment is filed with the court.

How to tell if a change of circumstances is *material* enough to convince a judge to change orders.

It wouldn't be fair to try to begin a list of every conceivable change of circumstances. The list is inexhaustible. You'll want expert advice on this subject. The list can be so long and so complicated, there's no way to know whether a specific scenario is likely to persuade a judge to change orders unless you first have an expert's understanding of your situation. Some things seem obvious. If one parent is jailed, or dies, the other parent presumably gets custody of the children. If the income of one or both parents changes dramatically, modifications in the child support are likely appropriate. If a parent consistently forgets to put a child's homework in his backpack for midweek visitation, may adjustments be made? Hmm… Important, yes, but not nearly as compelling. Or changes may occur if one parent gets involved in a gang, becomes dependent on drugs, or starts bringing around the children a felon with drug convictions. Any of those will cause a judge to reason the child's safety is at risk. As you can see, the possible deviations from "normal" co-parenting scenarios are endless.

Remember, working out an agreement is usually your best option. Sometimes you can work it out and sometimes you can't. When you can't work it out, a motion will be needed so a judge can weigh in.

Support enforcement: when a parent doesn't pay support.

If your ex-spouse knows about an order, has the ability to pay the support it requires, but does not, she is committing a crime. Jail is a last resort, of course, but a resort nonetheless. Jail time happens when the accused is convicted of contempt and a judge thinks jail time is appropriate. Usually a judge will figure it's better to have the parent free to work though. In an effort to collect support, the paycheck of a parent with a regular job can be *garnished* by special court order, even if the parent's employer is in another state. A support-withholding order (literally ORDER/NOTICE TO WITHHOLD…) is a court order that goes to the employer. It requires the employer to withhold the employee's earnings for support. Currently, the money is then sent a State Disbursement Unit, which then forwards payment to the parent who is owed the support.

It is important to file a motion to modify your child support if there is a significant change of your circumstances. I know of a case where a father was unemployed for years and filed nothing with the court to adjust the child support he owed. Because of that, the father was responsible for the *whole amount* of back child support owed *as it had originally been ordered*. The court did not have the ability to go backwards in time and adjust the father's payment amount to take into consideration his lost job. These days when so many people have lost their jobs, it's important to know courts' limitations. The judge was sympathetic, but the law tied his hands.

A private attorney like me can help with many of these functions. Sometimes, though, there's nothing like the clout of a powerful government agency to get the desired support enforcement. The Department of Child Support Services (DCSS), a California state agency, can take steps to (a) suspend an offender's driver's license, (b) prevent an offender from obtaining or renewing a passport, and (c) intercept a tax refund. The agency's services are free. The agency doesn't officially *represent* anyone. If the payer is in another state, do not fret. Each state is required to have an agency that is much like California's DCSS. In fact, the DCSS routinely enlists the help of states' counterpart agencies.

Moving away.
A standard provision in any permanent custody order in California is **"Neither parent may change the residence of the minor child or children outside the county without the written consent of the other parent or further order of the Court."**

San Diego County sees more than an average number of *move-away* requests because of the large number of military service members. Service members are transferred, rotated to different duty stations or separate from the military and want to return home to somewhere other than San Diego, His ex-spouse may have decided she'd like to stick around. Or vice versa.

If you find yourself in a move-away situation, don't move away with the children first and then hope for forgiveness from the court. I have handled more than a few cases where a parent did just that—moved first, thinking forgiveness could be had after the fact—and then came to me for damage control. *Moving is a big deal.* Make sure you do it the right way. Get your ducks in a row long before you move or, if you're a nonmoving parent, gear up to oppose the move if you want to change custody. A parent who moves away with the children without first getting a court order allowing the move never endears himself to a judge.

When a primary custodial parent needs to relocate, he must jump through several important hoops to get permission from a judge, unless of course the other parent signs off (literally) on the move. A signed, written agreement can substitute for a court order.

There are a number of reasons parents need to move. Among them are their own job-related reasons and their new spouses' job-related reasons, which may include military duty station reassignments. When a move is imminent, a motion is filed. A court then weighs any request by the nonmoving parent that it consider a change of child custody, or any motion by the moving parent that it grant an order allowing the move. Move-away motions are the stuff of highest drama in family court. Often, moves drastically reduce children's contact with nonmoving parents. In cases of interstate moves, drastic effects are the norm.

Move-away proceedings involve the highest level of conflict, at least in my experience over two decades of litigating in family court. But often, parents feel they have no choice other than to risk that conflict. They feel they must, at great cost, promote or oppose a move. Add to that the fact that no one wants to be found in violation of a court order (by moving without the court's okay, or by moving without the written permission of the nonmoving parent), and you get the absolute necessity of the move-away motion. The conflict level is exacerbated by the fact that a judge's decision about a very long-distance move feels like an all-or-nothing decision. It is. Either the child moves with the parent, or custody changes.

There have been two watershed cases on this issue in the last fifteen years that reached the California Supreme Court: *Burgess* **and** *La Musga*. Move-away cases can be extremely complex. Parents try to persuade judges that the facts compel them to agree with their positions. Anyone considering proposing or opposing a move-away motion would do well to get legal advice early—several months in advance of an anticipated move.

EPILOGUE

Congratulations! You now have a better idea about the ins and outs of family court in California. Most of the horror stories heard at cocktail parties and elsewhere about experiences in family court are directly traceable to clients not having enough information. When coupled with the stress of the moment and the urgent sense that something must be done right now, the too-frequent result is unfortunate decision making.

You're learning so you can plan and prepare for the inevitable highs and lows that result from family court crises. Don't assume you know enough. My favorite family law practice guide, something like the flat-rate manual used in an auto shop, is about two thousand pages long. And it's written for lawyers who already have a working understanding of family court! You've made a start here, but only a start.

The big ideas presented here are not that hard to remember, but let's recap anyway.

Here's a summary:
1. **Get good information early and often.** Things like knowing where and when to file a case are vital. Filing divorce in California a year after your

estranged spouse moves to Texas with the children probably is going to cause piecemeal litigation – some here, some there in Texas. If you can't afford a lawyer, there are several low-cost and free alternatives. The Family Law Facilitator's Office is a prime example. First come, first served; good, free help in every family court in the county. Downside: no one actually represents you in court or provides you with blow-by-blow coaching and education, and you have to draft your own documents. There are also Legal Aid and local volunteer lawyer programs. Check your county's Superior Court website for additional resources and information.

2. **Gather information, then take action, not the other way around.** Sometimes you won't know you need to act swiftly until you've gotten the information that leads you to that conclusion. Still, to act **effectively**, you've got to be well informed. If your spouse is preparing to leave the state with the children and there are no court orders forbidding it, you might not know a judge would find this to be an emergency and would put a stop to it unless you had read it here or elsewhere.

3. **Know what's important to family court judges, even if that means leaving out parts of your story that are important to you.** You should have some ideas about what is and is not important in court after having read this guide.

4. **Think about how your decisions are going to affect life six months from now and beyond.** Imagine that the dust has settled. A new routine for the

entire family is in place. What does that look like? How have the decisions you're contemplating affected that vision? Keeping this perspective will help you look past the hurt, anger and disappointment you feel in the painful present.

ABOUT THE AUTHOR

Paul Staley practices Family Law and Bankruptcy Law in San Diego, California. He lives there with his wife, Kathleen and their dogs, King and Goldie. They enjoy good movies, good music and great food. Paul enjoys playing his piano, singing with the church band and skiing whenever he can.

www.ingramcontent.com/pod-product-compliance
Lightning Source LLC
Chambersburg PA
CBHW051325170526
45166CB00002B/690